THE PATH
of
SOUL LIBERATION

THE PATH of SOUL LIBERATION

By Roy Eugene Davis

CSA PRESS, PUBLISHER
LAKEMONT, GA. 30552

Copyright © 1975 by
Roy Eugene Davis

Standard Book Number 0-87707-152-7

Library of Congress Catalog Number 75-2507

Printed in the United States of America
by CSA Printing and Bindery, Inc.

I salute the supreme teacher, the Truth,
whose nature is bliss, who is the giver
of the highest happiness, who is pure
wisdom, who is beyond all qualities and
infinite like the sky, who is beyond words,
who is one and eternal, pure and still,
who is beyond all change and phenomena
and who is the silent witness to all our
thoughts and emotions—I salute Truth,
the supreme teacher.

—Ancient Vedic Hymn

CONTENTS

Preface 9

Self-Knowledge 11

Summation 55

Glossary 71

PREFACE

The collection of verses offered here comprise the classic statements of the renowned philosopher-seer, Shankaracharya (Shankara). His original work is titled *Atmabodha,* or *Self-Knowledge,* and is considered one of the clearest views ever presented regarding the philosophy of Nondualism; the teaching that One Essence manifests as the total world-process.

These opening remarks are intentionally brief so that the reader might immediately begin a systematic study of the text itself. One is encouraged to approach this work with a calm and open mind, and to be willing to study, analyze and contemplate the meaning and import of the material. In Sanskrit, philosophy is called *darshana,* derived from the root word which means, *to see.* The purpose of philosophy, then, is to enable the student to see Truth directly. Speculation is natural to the process, but the result of such speculation should be actual realization or knowledge.

In this text *Self* does not mean the personality-self; it means that aspect of Pure Consciousness which has become identified with mind and is known, thereafter, as the soul. *Self-knowledge* is realization of the true nature. With this realization comes the automatic understanding of the cosmic process.

I have paraphrased the verses, using English equivalents for Sanskrit terms, without taking liberties with the original text and without compromising the meaning and, I hope, beauty and power. A few commonly used Sanskrit words are used in the commentary itself, and in each instance they are defined for clarification. In addition, a short summary of philosophical views has been appended and will be relevant to the overall message of the book. Finally, for the convenience of persons interested in the meanings of basic Sanskrit words and terms, a glossary will be found in the remaining pages. An understanding of this ancient language is not absolutely essential to the study of *Self-Knowledge,* but can serve as a helpful adjunct. There are many books which are now widely read in which the authors have made copious use of Sanskrit, therefore, it may be that the glossary will prove to be helpful in further studies.

—Roy Eugene Davis
December 23, 1974

SELF-KNOWLEDGE

1. I am composing this treatise on Self-Knowledge to serve the needs of those who have been purified through the practice of spiritual disciplines, who are peaceful in heart, free from (selfish) cravings and desirous of liberation.

Treatise, is a precise and entirely appropriate word used in respect to this masterly book of instruction; it is literally a formal and methodical exposition of the principles leading to knowledge of the Self, or soul.

Knowledge of the Self, or Self-Realization, is the reason for our spiritual practices. The soul, it is taught, is an individualization of Pure Consciousness. Self-Knowledge is the clear self-awareness of the truth about our essential nature. We are not to think in terms of acquiring realization, but of awakening to it. We are not to think in terms of developing a state of soul consciousness or of building it up, but to clear away the obscuring matters which prevent natural and spontaneous recognition of the truth. Shankara states in this first verse that he is writing, not to the one in whom the impulse toward realization has not arisen, but to "those who have been purified through the practice of spiritual disciplines, who are peaceful in heart, free from (selfish) cravings and desirous of liberation." We are, therefore, addressing ourselves to those who are ripe for the enlightenment experience.

Six *treasures*, according to master-teachers, form the ethical foundation of a truly spiritual life. Their practice prepares the inner faculties for the cultivation of higher knowledge. They are: *calmness of mind and being; self-control and discipline of the senses; contentment as the result of being inwardly settled; patience, regardless of what transpires about us; proper contemplation on the nature of Reality; and pure faith in the Life Process once its nature has been understood.* In addition, we are counseled to use our powers of discrimination, be free of attachments and yearn for liberation of consciousness. If we are true to ourselves and, therefore, true to life, we will realize the goal in the most efficient manner. Discipline, for our purposes, means: to synchronize thinking, feeling and intelligent action so as to be successful in our ventures with a minimum of wasted energy and time. Unless one is sincere on the path, unless one is totally dedicated to the ideal of experiencing the highest realization, random attempts are practically useless. No real guru will spend precious time with a person who is not yet committed to the enlightenment experience.

2. As fire (heat) is the direct cause of cooking, so knowledge and not any other form of discipline, is the direct cause of liberation; for liberation cannot be attained without knowledge.

If one's goal is to cook food, heat must be used, or something which results in the cooking process. Here, even though disciplines have been mentioned earlier, we are given the forthright information: "Liberation cannot be attained without knowledge." Knowledge, or full comprehension, about the nature of the Life Process Itself. Sages speak of higher knowledge and of lower knowledge. The former refers to comprehension of the subtle causes behind outer effects; the latter to comprehension of happenings in the relative worlds. To experience only, is not to have knowledge. One might taste food yet know not the real essence of the food, one might drive an automobile yet know not how it is manufactured, or even functions. One may feel an attunement with Life but not really know what Life is all about.

Knowledge is the result of the correct use of the faculty of intelligence; the ability to discriminate, or tell the difference between what is true about the object under analysis versus what we only assume to be true. The intuitive faculty is also useful, for it is the soul's way of knowing by knowing; no "reasons" need be present to support such knowing. Intuitive perception is always accurate, it is not like the vague assumptions, or convenient conclusions, at which we sometimes arrive to satisfy an emotional need.

The major point here set forth is that disciplines, while useful in clearing mind and emotional nature and in training us to use our abilities correctly, are not the cause of enlightenment. Enlightenment is the result of awakening to the realization of the truth about life. Hence, knowledge is automatic and liberation is spontaneous.

3. Action cannot destroy ignorance, for it is not in conflict with ignorance. Knowledge alone destroys ignorance, as light destroys dense darkness.

Ignorance, as used here, does not mean lack of education. It refers to our assuming that the world is real by itself, rather than a manifestation of the One Life. As long as we persist in operating from the level of understanding which assumes the world to be a mechanical multi-combination phenomenon and that we are but bodies moving through time and space, our actions, whatever they might be, are doomed to failure relative to our eventual experience of enlightenment. One who works from an understanding of causation and who thinks, "I am the doer," is self-deceived. It is only by moving into the transcendental level of awareness that one is able to see clearly and be possessed of perfect understanding.

4. **It is only because of ignorance that the Supreme Consciousness appears as finite. When ignorance is destroyed, the Supreme Consciousness which does not admit of any multiplicity whatsoever, truly reveals Itself by Itself, like the sun when the cloud is removed.**

When one is deluded and does not clearly comprehend the nature of Life, from subtle to gross expression, only the finite aspect of creation is observed and believed to be real of itself. When, through discrimination and intuitive meditation practice, one transcends mental concepts one directly perceives the truth. Then Supreme Consciousness "reveals Itself by Itself." Consciousness is self-luminous and requires nothing external to Itself. It is "the light that lighteth every man" who comes into the world. This essential essence, the soul or Self, is referred to by members of the Christian faith as the indwelling Christ.

5. **Through steady practice, knowledge purifies the embodied soul stained by ignorance, and then itself disappears, as a purifying agent disappears after it has cleansed the water.**

Of course, the soul does not need to be purified. What is meant here is that the soul's coverings, or sheaths, are

Self-Knowledge 15

purified as one remains steady in Realization. In the early stages there is usually a taint of delusion remaining, so that one who intutitively realizes the truth about Life is still under the conviction that he is realizing; that is, "I am not Knowledge Itself, I am perceiving the truth about life." In the course of time, through "steady practice," energies flowing from the transcendental Source infiltrate the mental field and the nervous system, resulting in cleansing and purification. Finally the consciousness *of* Knowledge disappears and only the Transcendental Existence remains. It just is; It does not enjoy Its beingness, for this would be evidence of duality, calling for yet more purification.

6. **The world, filled with attachments and aversions, and the rest, is like a dream: it appears to be real as long as one is ignorant, but becomes unreal when one is awake.**

This is a classic explanation. Dreams are common to all of us and can be understood in this context. Our dreams are totally the product of our own mental processes. It has even been said that dreams are "memories" which become active and influenced by subconscious urges and impressions. Sometimes, dreams are creative but the dream-material is still of the mind. Mystics teach that the average person, even when awake to the sense-perceived world, is like one in a dream; he does not see clearly because he does not use his intellectual faculty correctly, and he "projects," or assumes, instead of getting to the truth. He is also at the mercy of inherited tendencies, early impressions, social conditioning and peer-group influence. Also, because he is not anchored in the Self he either tends to grasp at things, or rejects them; thus, he is caught up in the seeming never-ending process of nature. The ebb and flow of energy, the setting and reaching of goals, the inter-relationships between things and other life-forms—these are natural to the relative plane of existence. The Sanskrit word for this phenomenon is *samsara,* and its natural trend is to continue. As long as one is identified with this trend, one is sure to continue in the waking-dream experience. But, when one awakens to the truth about Life and sees clearly the *why* and the *how* of it all, the relative world is no longer real in the sense of its having independent support.

7. The world appears to be real as long as nondual Consciousness, which is the basis of all (manifestation), is not known. It is like any other illusion, having no basis of its own.

Non-dual Consciousness is the true support of the phenomenal universe. When we conclude that the universe is without support and see only the various expressions of relative nature, we miss the point, or we draw a false conclusion. Seeing an inanimate object in the dark, for instance, we may assume it is something else. If the "something else" we assume it to be represents a threat to our well-being, we will react emotionally, even though no real threat exists. My guru, Paramahansa Yogananda, used to say, "The universe is God's dream; it is all taking place in God's mind." From the point of view of God's mind we can see that the universe, which seems so obvious to sense perceptions, is truly a dream-happening. Therefore, Supreme Consciousness is the primal cause, as well as the sole support of the universe. When we realize this, the universe will not truly vanish from our sight, but we will see it in a new and different light. It will no longer be the fearsome, or misunderstood, forever flowing happening we have heretofore presumed it to be. It will be Supreme Consciousness appearing *as* the world. Supreme Consciousness, through the process of self-modification, extends as the

Self-Knowledge 17

universes and all that inhabits them. The universe, then, is the result of the play of Consciousness.

8. **All the various forms exist in the imagination of the perceiver, the substratum (supporting principle) being the eternal and all-pervading Consciousness (in partial manifestation) whose nature is Existence and Intelligence. Names and forms are like rings and bracelets and Consciousness is like the gold from which they are formed.**

The meaning of "the various forms exist in the imagination of the perceiver" is that the names, or labels, we give to the various forms are ours and do not belong to the forms themselves. No matter what we elect to call a thing, it is we who have thus labeled it. The thing itself is a manifestation of Consciousness in Its temporary and relative form. Pure Consciousness is without attributes, but when moving in the direction of outward manifestation, takes on characteristics and attributes. Existence there always is, and Intelligence is the aspect of Consciousness which directs the universal process. We refer to a piece of gold, used as a body ornament, as a ring, a bracelet, or whatever best describes its use; the names are ours, the object remains what it is, gold.

9. **As the all-prevading space appears to vary on account of its association with various forms (mental, electric, magnetic) which are different from each other, and (again) remains pure upon the destruction of the form-giving qualities, so also the omnipresent Lord (Consciousness as creative manifesting power) appears to be diverse on account of His association with various form-building qualities and remains pure and One upon the dissolution of these qualities.**

We can examine this verse on at least two different levels of understanding. Space is broken up, to our vision, by the various objects existing in a given space that is perceived. Yet, if the objects were to be removed, space would remain. Space is not *distance,* space is that in which things rest and happenings occur. Distance is a measurement from one point in space to another. Space is a field in which the universe happens. Time-sense is due to our changing our perspective. To some, time seems to flow; we have past, present and future. Time, space, light particles and energy—make up the basic substance of which the manifest realms are expressed. The Sanskrit word for this basic substance, a modification of Consciousness, is *maya. Maya* is not an illusion; but our taking it to be real, that is, to have independent existence, constitutes for the sense of illusion. This is the basic cause of delusion, ignorance, or self-forgetfulness. When *maya* is dissolved, Consciousness will remain. This is the second level of understanding and is clearly realized when the transcendental level of Consciousness is realized. Even before realization is ours, we can use our intelligence, our faculty of discernment, to be reminded of the true nature of the Life Process.

10. **Owing to Its association with various restricting qualities and attributes, such ideas as differences (between people), color, and social position are superimposed on Supreme Consciousness; as flavor, color and worth are attributed to water.**

During deep meditation, and when we are active in the world while remaining soul-conscious, we are above mundane concerns regarding other people; their personality, skin color, or social status. We know that all people are souls expressing through the various bodies and minds; which are themselves conditioned. The outer is conditioned, the inner is the same in all human beings. One of the characteristics of a saint, it is said, is that a saint will see all people as being expressions of Consciousness and will accord them equal respect. With understanding we can see that everyone has a place in the cosmic scheme and that what is needed is to encourage individuals to find their true place and work out their personal destiny in harmony with the whole. Society, like Nature, is a continuum—a series of connected parts—and the health and well-being of the total organism is dependent upon the health and well-being of the individual.

11. **The physical body, the medium through which the soul experiences pleasure and pain, is determined by past actions and formed out of the five great subtle elements, which becomes gross matter when one-half portion of one subtle element becomes united with one-eighth of each of the other four.**

Seers teach that the body is not fully the effect of the union of our parents; there is also the matter of the soul's desire for physical expression. This desire is due to need, or craving, for sense-oriented experience. The need is due to the accumulation of subconscious impressions, or karmic patterns, which supply the motive force.

The subtle elements, five in number, are at first pure and not yet involved with manifestation. They are in rudimentary form. However, when they mix, grosser elements are expressed and involvement with, and *as* nature, is possible. The first element is said to be ether, the background of space; due to a mixture of Consciousness and Its modification, *maya*. From ether evolves air; from air, fire; from fire, water; from water, earth. Transmitted to the elements, from the Godhead, at the time of initial outflowing, are the three electric attributes which permeate all creation: *sattva*, *rajas, and tamas.* Simply, these terms mean: *sattva,* elevating and purifying attribute; *rajas,* neutralizing current, or attribute; *tamas,* gravity, inertia, or heaviness. The first and last relate to the positive and negative polarities, the middle attribute is the current flowing between them, resulting in balance.

The subtle elements are untainted, then become mixed, resulting in gross compounds. Combinations of subtle elements, in specific proportions, result in the production of gross elements. The verse states that each gross element consists of one-half portion of its subtle counterpart and one-eighth each of the four remaining subtle elements. For instance: One-half *subtle ether* and four one-eighth parts (amounting to one-half) of the remaining subtle elements results in the appearance of gross ether. One half portion of *subtle air* and four one-eighth parts of the remaining subtle elements results in the appearance of gross water. And, so on.

12. The subtle body, the instrument of the soul's experience, consists of the five divisions of prana, the ten organs (those of perception and action), the mind and the faculty of intelligence—all formed from rudimentary elements before their subdivision and combination with one another.

Vital force, *prana,* is divided into five parts according to their respective functions in nature: that part which is the basis for the rest; that part which functions in the body, moves downward and expels unassimilated food; that part which pervades throughout the body; that part which ascends in the body, allowing regurgitation, and assists the soul to depart the body when the time arrives; that part which enables the body to digest food and convert it into needed nutritional mixtures. As the three electric attributes (see above) make up nature, so the five *pranas* are derived from the *rajasic,* or neutralizing parts of the five subtle elements.

The organs of perception are the ears, skin, eyes, tongue, and nose. The organs of action are the hands, feet, speech apparatus, and organs of evacuation and generation. The five organs of perception are said to be formed from the *sattvic,* or elevating parts of the subtle elements, because this attribute has the characteristic of brightness. The organs of action are believed to be formed of the *rajasic* parts of the subtle elements, because they are active and allow the embodied soul to reach goals, satisfy desires, and neutralize desire patterns.

Mind is considered to be produced from the *sattvic* parts of the five subtle elements, and is that function which enables one to consider different viewpoints about a given subject. In modern metaphysical circles a definition of the human mind is: "an individualization of Cosmic Mind." Mind is considered to be the creative medium which makes possible the appearance of the world, and the intentional modification of it. Another aspect of the mind is the *intellectual* faculty. This enables one to discern the true nature and character of an object analyzed. Another characteristic of the mind is that it tends to seek pleasurable experiences. This can have survival value as most survival activities (eating, sleeping, succeeding in ventures, communicating well with others, etc.) are pleasurable. A problem can arise, however, if one seeks pleasure for the sake of pleasure, instead of merely enjoying pleasure as an adjunct to survival experience. One is likely to seek pleasure at the cost of health, social stability, or even peace of mind. The final characteristic of the mind is egoity, the sense of I-consciousness. When we understand what the "I" really is, we are enlightened; when we assume that the "I" is a separate and important (by itself) entity, we are in trouble.

13. **Consciousness-*maya* (which is the cause of unknowing), indescribable and beginningless, is called the cause or restriction superimposed on Supreme Consciousness. Know for certain (however) that Supreme Consciousness is other than (and not really restricted by) the three vehicles of the soul (causal, astral and physical).**

We cannot describe Consciousness as having a beginning because it is the root-cause of everything, the first cause, the only cause. We cannot fully describe It, however we may try, because the mind which perceives It is, itself, a product or an effect. The Self, the realized soul, can know the truth about Consciousness but as long as the realized soul is working through a mind there must remain a thin veil of delusion. *Maya,* though a self-modification of Consciousness, veils the perception of ultimate truth from one involved with *maya*. This self-modification is essential to the purpose of creation, for without it, Consciousness could not become manifest and the world-process could not exist. Supreme Consciousness, that aspect which is without modification or attributes, is other than the subtle vehicles of the soul and is not restricted by them at all.

The three vehicles of the soul here mentioned are: causal, astral, physical. The causal body is formed of the aforementioned divisions of *prana,* or vital force, and is possessed of the *inner organs,* of a subtle nature, which are later expressed through astral and physical forms. The astral body is made up of grosser energies and sustained by a "heart" which pumps vital force throughout. The astral eye is the *single eye,* or the third eye. It is not an eye as we know a physical eye to be; it is a center of perception. It is also the distribution point through which down-flowing vital forces enter the astral and the physical bodies. Vital force flows down from the *crown chakra* in, and above, the higher brain area.

The Self, which is individualized Pure Consciousness, is likewise independent of the three bodies. Here is a subtle point; the Self is described as above, and is referred to as a soul only when identified with the mind and is, then, as a result, deluded. It is the soul-aspect of Consciousness which struggles, experiences in the world, and yearns for knowledge. The Self-aspect is ever free, even though individualized.

14. **On account of union with the five sheaths, the Supreme Consciousness appears to be like them, as is the case with a crystal, which appears to be endowed with such colors as blue or red (or any color, depending upon the color source) when in contact with a blue or red background.**

The author of this treatise stands firm in his exposition of eternal truths. Since Pure Consciousness is the cause of the subtle and gross elements, It cannot be them. Because of temporary identification it seems to reflect the characteristics of gross matter. The bodies, or vehicles, used by the Self, are sometimes referred to as *sheaths;* the Self uses the bodies, but wears them for a purpose. When a body ceases to function the Self continues to fulfill needed destiny.

15. **One should, through discrimination, separate the pure and inmost Consciousness from the sheaths by which It is covered, as one separates grain from the covering husk (or covering).**

There are several ways which are taught to seekers as

possible ways to liberation of consciousness. *Hatha Yoga* practices insures health and correct body function, and prepares one for the awakening and ascent of *kundalini:* the aspect of the vital force that usually resides in a dormant condition, until aroused, when it then ascends through the *chakra system* and becomes stablized at the *crown chakra*. During this time-process internal changes are experienced, vital centers are quickened, the mind is made steady and eventually the transcendental experience is had. *Karma Yoga* is the way of selfless action; which insures that no more desires bind one to the future, presently active subconscious patterns can be handled and neutralized, and dormant ones dissolved. *Bhakti Yoga* is the way of personal surrender to God and the worship of God; which can lead to the transcendental experience. It can also lead to emotionalism and involvement in powerful feelings. *Raja Yoga* (the "royal" way) is the way of meditation; through mind regulation, concentration, and the transcendental experience. *Jnana Yoga* is the way of Self-Knowledge through the discernment process; it is the most subtle, but the safest way of all because it enables the practitioner to see clearly the nature of the Life process and does not accept any emotion, theory, or opinion which bars direct comprehension. There are other "yogas" but they are variations of these basic and traditional paths.

16. Though all-pervading, Supreme Consciousness does not shine in everything; It is manifest only in the organ of intelligence, like a reflection in clear water, or in a stainless mirror.

The *organ of intelligence* is almost clear, or translucent, and allows light to pass through. Because of this it is through the organ of intelligence that Supreme Consciousness is known. It is not clearly known through the other

Self-Knowledge

organs of the mind because the other organs serve other purposes and are not suitable for the transmission of Pure Knowledge. Supreme Consciousness pervades everything as the support and underlying being of all. Because the faculty of intelligence is an aspect of the mind, and the mind is composed of "mixed" elements, when the Light of the Supreme is cognized through intelligence then the one who is realizing the Supreme is defined as a soul.

17. **Realize individualized Supreme Consciousness to be distinct from the body, sense organs, mind, intelligence and non-differentiated primal-nature; It is the witness of their functions and the ruler of them.**

When resting in the full realization of our Real Nature, we know we are not any of the coverings, nor are we anything of a material nature. We use the term "material" to designate anything manifested, from subtle to gross levels; we use the term "physical" to mean the substance of the world we know through sense perception.

18. **As the moon appears to be moving when the clouds move in the sky, so also, to the nondiscriminating, individualized Supreme Conscousness appears to be active when in reality only the senses are active.**

Obviously, the impression that we sometimes have of the moon moving when only the clouds are moving, is due to faulty sense perception, however rational it may seem. Likewise, when the senses are active and we are caught up in the surge of feelings and thoughts, we assume the soul is restless and similarly caught up. We then say, "I am restless." "I am confused." Or, "I am sick." None of these can be really true of the Self, even if true of the body and mind. When we can rest in the conscious realization of our

Real Nature, which is ever stable and bright, this realization can extend into the mental field and the physical body and healing is the effect.

19. The body, senses, mind and intelligence engage in their respective activities with the help of Consciousness, which is inherent in the individualized Supreme Consciousness, just as men work with the help of light that is inherent in the sun.

We are able to function and to operate through our bodies and sense organs because the light of Pure Consciousness infiltrates and nourishes. It would be foolish to state that without It we would not be able to function, *for without It we would not exist*. It is wise for us to use our mind and body intelligently, but we should never forget our basic nature as Consciousness, and that we are working *through* and not *as* a body, only.

20. Foolish people, through nondiscrimination, superimpose upon the stainless Supreme Consciousness which is Existence and Consciousness Absolute, the characteristics and functions of the body and senses, just as people attribute such traits as blueness and the appearance of curved space to the sky.

The author of these verses was skilled at debating with representatives of other philosophical schools and, therefore, is methodical in his repeated emphasis concerning the nature of Supreme Consciousness as being clear and untouched by any of the characteristics of nature. While this may seem repetitious to the casual reader, let us be reminded that it can serve a purpose, and tends to anticipate questions which might come from different persons at different times. By "foolish," is meant being weak in intellectual powers. One without the capacity, or the inclination, to correctly use the faculty of discernment is almost certain to draw incorrect conclusions when examining any problem.

21. **As the movement that belongs to water is (sometimes) attributed, through ignorance, to the moon which is reflected in it, so also, enjoyment and other limitations which belong to the mind, are falsely attributed to Supreme Consciousness.**

Here we touch on what is a sensitive subject to many people, that of experiencing enjoyment. On the one hand a teacher will be heard to say, "Self-Realization brings lasting joy and never-ending bliss." On the other hand, teachers of liberation through Self-Knowledge stress that enjoyment is made possible because of the mind and ego-sense. A liberated person, to the eyes of one who observes him, is happy and content, but notions of "how good it feels" to be enlightened does not enter his mind. That is, he is not motivated by the urge to enjoy, or the need to enjoy, anymore than he is given to actions which will result in pain and limitation. One who is established in the realization of the Self experiences a bliss which is independent of sensory organs. In many philosophical systems the mind is considered to be an extra sensory organ, because impressions are received by it and interpreted by it.

22. **Attachment, desire, pleasure, pain and other misguiding urges and reactions, are perceived to exist as long as intelligence and mind functions. They are not perceived in deep sleep when the mind is no longer cognized. Therefore, they belong to the mind and not to Supreme Consciousness.**

The first sentence of this verse refers to the ordinary

waking state. It is true that we also experience a variety of feelings and urges during dreams. However, during dreamless sleep we identify more closely with the subtle vehicle of the soul and experience a detachment from the mental functions. This is why dreamless sleep is used as a crude comparison with the transcendental experience. Not that dreamless sleep, as a forever condition, is the ideal—only that one can analyze the condition and draw the conclusion that when attention is withdrawn from sensory organs and mental activities, a type of peace and serenity is realized. Also, at this time all problems vanish and all sense of difference recedes.

23. The nature of Supreme Consciousness is eternity, purity, reality, awareness and bliss, just as luminosity is the nature of the sun, coolness of water and heat of fire.

The natural condition of Pure Consciousness is as described and are not qualities or imposed characteristics. When an enlightened person says, "My nature is bliss," he is stating a truth. He is not blissful because he has attained the spiritual heights, but because the nature of unrestricted awareness *is* bliss. Such bliss is not an emotion, or a feeling, in the common sense, it is the nature of Supreme Consciousness.

24. Such a notion as "I know" is produced by the union, due to nondescrimination, of a modification of the mind with the two (manifest) aspects of Supreme Consciousness, namely existence and self-awareness.

It is taught that Supreme Consciousness remains ever unattached to *maya*, the subtle fabric of the relative worlds, even though It works through it. The wave action of the mind is referred to as a modification. The memory of a past experience, or previously observed object, as well as present perceptions, stimulates one or more of the electric attributes inherent in the mind. This starts a wave which gives rise to notions such as "I now know," or "I am happy." So it is not due to direct perception of the truth about Life that mental activity is initiated. To truly see life happenings as they are, is to be the thoughtless observer and to be content here and now. To be identified with memories, or overly involved with present happenings, is to be dependent upon externals and to be open to such influences. This is why even-mindedness is recommended as an essential for one seeking liberation. To have a mind which is even, in which waves do not interfere, is not to be uncaring; it is to be the observer, always balanced, always centered and composed.

25. **Supreme Consciousness never undergoes change and the faculty of intelligence is never endowed with consciousness (of its own). But man believes Supreme Consciousness to be identical with the faculty of intelligence and falls under such delusions as that he is the seer and the knower.**

Change is characteristic of the relative planes, not of the non-dual Pure Consciousness. The faculty of intelligence, being an organ of perception, is formed of the stuff of nature; it is not conscious, any more than the mind or body is conscious. It is Supreme Consciousness which shines through nature. It alone is conscious and as it expresses through nature we sometimes falsely assume that objects in nature have independent consciousness. Assumptions give rise to delusions.

26. **The soul, regarding itself as an individualized living being, is overcome by fear, just like a man who regards a rope as a snake (when he sees it in a dim light). The**

soul regains fearlessness by realizing It (the soul) is not an individualized entity but the Supreme Consciousness.

We have often stated that the soul *is* an individualization of Supreme Consciousness. This definition is given in general classes and books meant for wide readership because it comes close to the actual condition. The majority of seekers who are new on the path are not yet endowed with sufficient analytical powers to discern the true nature of things. In some scriptures soul is defined as "individualized Pure Consciousness which has become identified with nature." In other commentaries soul is defined as "the *reflection* of Pure Consciousness in the mind." In this latter definition one is asked to imagine a moon, and its many reflections in many bodies of water. The reflections are not the moon itself, anymore than the reflection of Supreme Consciousness is Consciousness Itself.

Fears and all emotional reactions are due to our accepting the false notion that Life is not one, but many. In this verse the author is not suggesting that we not be observant concerning our relationships in the relative world, or that we not be practical. The rope-snake reference is used to point out how we often tend to react to what we think is before us instead of what is actually there. Due to the mixture of tendencies and attributes in nature, and people, while we are functioning in the relative world we must use common sense. Wisdom should always take the upper hand in our relationships.

27. **The mind, sense-organs and other body-parts, are illumined by Supreme Consciousness alone, as a jar or a pot by a lamp (receives the light of the lamp). But these material objects cannot illumine themselves.**

Again the point is made that it is the light of Supreme

Self-Knowledge 31

Consciousness that makes possible all seeming external lights. We might here consider the matter of liberation of consciousness. Liberation refers to freedom from bondage. As long as we are deluded into thinking that we are restricted, we are in need of liberation. Some schools teach that liberation is the result of a long difficult journey through various times and spaces, incarnation after incarnation. This is how it seems to be, to some. But, it is not essential that one look forward to "working out" his salvation by confronting karmic debts and building a spiritual consciousness. That we must be practical and learn to handle subconscious patterns, is obvious. To think of building a spiritual consciousness is ignorance, for this implies further conditioning and further modification of the mental aspect of the body's nature. Spiritual consciousness is the result of awakening and knowledge; it is not the result of conditioning the mind. Liberation is possible only when Consciousness is detached from the mind, or when the point of view is changed from being a mind to resting in the awareness of the true Self. To an aware seeker who is intent upon liberation, any practice which does not result in freedom is to be avoided—any speculative philosophical systems that are offered to pacify mind, or settle the emotions by imparting false information, is a waste of time.

28. As a lighted lamp does not need another lamp to manifest its light, so the Supreme Consciousness does not need another instrument of consciousness to illumine Itself.

Supreme Consciousness is self-effulgent. It is the Light of lights. It is That by which all is made possible. It alone is Real (permanent and changeless), all else is unreal (subject to change). We are not here saying that sense-perceived objects are not discernible to the one who perceives them. They are "real" in that context. Seers speak of Consciousness as being Real and not in need of another support; all else we might observe is either a reflection, or an extension, of Consciousness.

29. By negating all restricting appearances through the help of scriptural statement, "It (Supreme Consciousness) is not this (the appearance), It is not this (whatever else might be perceived)," realize the oneness of the Self as Supreme Consciousness by means of the great affirmations and statements of the seers.

A scripture is not a mere book of philosophical speculation; it is revealed truth, given by enlightened sages who speak clearly of the essential nature of Life and the world. We are advised to counteract negative mental impressions and see through the appearances of the world by affirming that which is true. By affirmation we do not mean repetition of a formula, or phrase, to condition the mind; we mean to take a statement which contains the essence of what is true and dwell on it until our own realization is experienced. One way is to be reminded that no matter what we observe, from the vantage point of being an observer, cannot be our true nature. Nor can that which is observed be Supreme Consciousness; for It is experienced and not observed. The "help of a scriptural statement" is useful advice, for by contemplating the meaning behind such statements we are correctly instructed and our dormant awareness of the truth is awakened. This is why repeated study is recommended. A reader who scans this book once, or twice, and then moves on to one which is more "interesting," or "exciting," will be missing the point of the book's existence. Not that several scriptures should not be studied, but they are to be carefully and repeatedly examined.

Self-Knowledge

30. The body, mind and all modifications of them, created by Consciousness-*maya* and of the nature of objects, are perishable like bubbles. Realize through discrimination that you are the stainless Supreme Consciousness, completely apart from them.

All manifest things will one day pass away. As long as we persist in accepting ourselves as a thing, we will suffer pain and live in fear of eventual death. When we realize our nature to be Pure Consciousness, we can function in the world with understanding and in perfect peace. We *are*, already, Supreme Consciousness. This is our true nature, all the rest is the result of outer identification. When we affirm, with understanding, "This Self is Supreme Consciousness," we are not trying to take the place of God; we are merely affirming the truth. When we affirm that we are limited human beings we are affirming something which is false. In this philosophical presentation God is considered to be the Oversoul, or Cosmic Soul. Beyond God is Supreme Consciousness. To many, they are one and the same, and to follow this line of thought we could say, "All of nature and Supreme Consciousness are one and the same." Consciousness can produce nature out of Itself, but nature cannot produce Consciousness.

In some yoga systems it is taught that the goal is union with God. To come into a conscious working relationship with God is certainly not an inferior ideal. Those intent upon liberation through knowledge also want to realize the final truth about the nature of Consciousness. As the soul is Consciousness reflected in the mind, so the Godhead is Consciousness reflected in Universal Mind. It is further taught that if the soul does reach the level of "union with God," when the universes are dissolved, if liberation is not experienced, the soul may well be expelled into the new universal process when the process begins once more.

31. I am free of changes which are the inherent characteristics of matter; for I am other than the body. I am unattached to the sense-objects for I (Supreme Consciousness) am without sense organs.

It is obvious that one would not be able to make this statement without sense organs. When we express verbally we must use the organ of speech. Here, however, is a statement indicating high realization and one to be affirmed and contemplated. Contemplation is the act of flowing attention to a given object, or theme, in order to discern the truth inherent in it. This statement is not one to superficially repeat, but one to inwardly acknowledge.

32. I am free from sorrow, attachment, malice and fear; for I am other than the mind. "He (Supreme Consciousness) is without breath and without mind, pure, higher than the high and imperishable."

Since Supreme Consciousness is free of identification with mind, It is also free of all the tendencies to which the mind is an heir. In the affirmation, "He" refers to Supreme Consciousness. Of course, in the pure state such designations as "he," or "she," do not accurately apply. Here a relative reference is used. The male aspect, or positive polarity, impregnates the female aspect, or negative polarity. The male gives, the female receives. In Eastern scriptures First Cause is designated as male because It is the initial activating influence. Nature, or creation, is referred to as female because nature is receptive and responsive. These are convenient terms, only. Since Pure Consciousness is not a person, no hint of supremacy relative to male, or female, characteristics is implied. "Higher than the high" refers to Supreme Consciousness as in contrast to It as manifesting as the Godhead. There is no great difference between Them;

Supreme Consciousness, is pure, or without attributes; the Godhead is Supreme Consciousness with attributes. Therefore, dual expressions of the same Thing.

33. **From Supreme Consciousness are born breath, mind and all organs of the senses; subtle matter, air, light, water and earth, and Supreme Consciousness supports them all.**

From the true Source is born, or is projected, all modifications and forms in the universe. Everything emerges from that primal Something, for things cannot come out of nothing. A magnetic field is produced, then from the negative polarity there flows a current which modifies as it becomes more gross, until the physical realms are manifested. *Tamas guna,* the electric attribute of inertia, makes this possible. *Sattva guna* is the positive polarity which eventually redeems the worlds. *Rajas guna,* the neutralizing current, makes possible the activity in nature and the eventual balancing of the pairs of opposites.

34. **I am without attributes and action, eternal and pure, free from stain and desire, changeless and formless and always free.**

Though everything in manifestation is possessed of attributes and is in motion, Pure Consciousness rests serene and free from Its outer projection. This verse is ideal for contemplation and will lead one to the experience of the transcendental plane.

35. **I fill all things, inside and out, like subtle matter-space. Changeless and the same in all, I am pure, unattached, stainless and immutable.**

Pervading everything, similar to space which is material, but not qualified as space is, Supreme Consciousness is the support of all that appears. It is not "above" this material plane in the sense that *above* is a direction upward; It resides at the inmost center of everything. Even within us, for we are advised by seers to "seek out the truth of existence in the heart." Heart here means the center, the core, the basis of things.

36. I am verily that Supreme Consciousness, which is eternal, stainless and free; which is One, indivisible and nondual; and which is of the nature of Bliss, Truth, Knowledge and Infinity.

One, in the sense that Supreme Consciousness is not related to anything else, It is the only Reality, Infinity, in that It is not identified with time. To paraphrase, one might say, "I will have no other Goal before me." Even when one is worshipping God, or an aspect of the Godhead, one can remember that behind the *form* is that which makes the form possible. Even though one listens, with respect, to one's teacher, or guru—one can remember that behind the form of the teacher, or guru, is that which makes them both possible.

37. The impression of "I am Supreme Consciousness," which comes as a result of uninterrupted reflection, destroys ignorance and its distractions, as a special medicine destroys disease.

The word "impression" is correct, for when one can state "I am Supreme Consciousness," it is the result of a mental impression even though realization is almost clear. If one were really nondual and transcendent one would not make the statement, one would merely *be*. Uninterrupted reflection, steady meditation and contemplation on the highest ideal, with devotion and yearning to know, has been extolled as the certain route to enlightenment. The "special medicine" referred to is an ancient concoction known to Vedic specialists, a compound of mercury and sulphur thought to contain powerful cleansing and restorative influences.

38. **Sitting in a solitary place, freeing the mind from desires, and controlling the senses, meditate with unswerving attention on the Infinite and Supreme Consciousness-Reality which is nondual.**

Qualified yoga teachers do not discredit other forms of meditation, but the emphasis here is contemplation on the non-dual aspect of Consciousness, in order to rise free of all possible restricting influences. The suggestion here is to practice meditation as explained in the *Yoga Sutras* of Patanjali: to free the mind from desires by purposely withdrawing attention and vital force from the senses, which is the practice of pranayama (control of vital forces); to be restrained, so that no temptation to flow outward remains; to concentrate, or focus the attention at one point; to continue this flowing of attention, or to meditate; then, to finally transcend identification and experience Pure Consciousness. This is a scientific, practical and result-getting procedure.

In this meditation procedure we even rise free of the electric attributes in the mind, and above the feeling nature; for as long as we retain identification with the electric attributes and the feeling nature, there is the possibility of mind-waves being generated. If we experience visions, strong feelings, or expanded states, we are still identified with the modifications of nature, no matter how "cosmic" the experience seems to be. So long as we retain identification with mind and feeling nature, whatever seems to be realization might well be an *impression* of realization; that is, we catch a glimpse of Truth but it then becomes reflected in the mind as an impression. We then tend to think in terms of partial-knowledge of the nature of Reality. This experience gives rise to the attitude expressed in the statement: "I feel I know the truth, but I am not sure I do."

39. The wise person should intelligently merge the entire objective world in Supreme Consciousness alone and constantly think of that Reality as the stainless sky.

Intelligently, that is with discernment, one should meditate and merge (dissolve) ideas of the world into the clear, non-dual aspect of Consciousness. As far as the eye can see, the clear sky has nothing which disturbs the perception; so one should consider Supreme Consciousness as being clear and without any pattern or form to obstruct It. This is known as meditating on the Absolute, or Pure Existence.

40. He who has attained the Supreme Goal discards all such objects as name and form, and dwells as the embodiment of Infinite Consciousness and bliss.

To discard name and form does not mean, in our society, to dramatize outer renunciation and cease to use names for things and to use objects without prudence; it means to see clearly, and forever realize, that names are for convenience and forms are to be wisely used, or related to. To cease to be attached to things, even while functioning intelligently in the world, is to be a renunciate of the highest order.

41. The Supreme Consciousness, because Its nature is exceeding bliss, does not admit to any distinction of the knower, knowledge, or the object of knowledge. It alone shines.

Self-Knowledge

Samadhi is a Sanskrit term meaning "to bring into even-ness." When the waves no longer arise in the mental field during meditation, the mind can be a clear reflector in which the Light of Consciousness can shine. As long as we are aware that we are experiencing, or that we know, we are still in a dualistic condition. This is the lower *samadhi*, or *savikalpa samadhi;* it is *samadhi* with mental support, or a seed image in the mind. The higher experience is *nirvikalpa samadhi;* that which is without mental support. If one is not satisfied with the lower *samadhi*, and continues to yearn for Knowledge, the mind will, in time, become purified and the higher *samadhi* will be experienced. Many meditators settle for less than the ultimate realization and are content to merge with an attribute of Consciousness; such as light, bliss, power, love, cosmic consciousness, and so on.

42. By constant meditation the flame of pure knowledge arises, which completely burns up the causes of ignorance.

The more we gain access to the realization of our true nature, the more we experience a transforming flow of energy, which has its origin in the transcendental field, and this neutralizaes and burns out seeds of karma and all latent mental impressions which restrict clear realization. Every time we come out of meditation and retain the awareness of the experience, we open ourselves to this flow of high-frequency energy which has a cleansing and redemptive effect upon the organism. It is also likely that kundalini will awaken and, when it does, powerful upward surges will enliven the system, cleanse the nerves, calm the mind and make meditation easier. Teachers of the way of Knowledge stress contemplation on the highest ideal, rather than overemphasis upon the other basic yogic practices. They know that with awakening all will work out well, and the internal processes will be spontaneous. If we yearn to really know the truth about life, and contemplate Supreme Consciousness, we will be led into the path which is best for us and Innate Intelligence will be the true guide.

43. As the sun appears after banishing of darkness by the coming of dawn, so Supreme Consciousness appears after the signs of ignorance have been dissolved by knowledge.

The "signs of ignorance" are the impressions, and obstructions, in the mental field. Pure Consciousness cannot be known as long as they remain, or until they are transcended in the quiet of meditation. Once steady realization of Pure Consciousness is a matter of course, delusion is banished entirely. There is then no danger of one ever falling back in unknowingness. However, as long as mental impressions remain, regardless of how high one might rise, there is the possibility of one's drifting from the former high resolve and becoming again entangled in the snare of the senses and in the confusion of thoughts. The positive impressions made on the mental field, by early intense practice of spiritual disciplines and meditations, will remain and eventually bring the person back on the path of conscious effort which can lead to realization. No gain is ever lost, no right attempt is ever wasted.

44. Though Supreme Consciousness is an ever-present reality, because of ignorance It is unrealized. When ignorance is dissolved then Supreme Consciousness is realized. Failure to realize Reality is often due to one's looking in the wrong place for it.

Even for one who is deluded and confused, the essential nature is always bright and shining, though not consciously realized. When one awakens from the "mortal dream," then Reality is known. One cannot realize the truth about Reality if one does not know where, or how, to look. The classic example given in this context is that of a woman who mistakenly thinks her necklace is lost, and looks frantically for it, not knowing it hangs around her neck all the while. It is true that we go the route of study, counsel, trial and error, and association with teachers and a guru. The real search is within, but outer aids can be useful. Wise teachers suggest: the best study is that of scripture; the best counsel is taken from fully realized persons; the best association is with a teacher, or guru, who is firmly established in the highest realization.

45. **Supreme Consciousness appears to be a soul because of (temporary) forgetfulness (on the part of the soul). This sense of individuality is banished when the real nature of the soul is realized.**

When Supreme Consciousness is reflected in a mental field and takes the reflection for the Real existence, then the Real existence is temporarily forgotten. "Temporary," because reflections eventually cease to be reflections when the Source of the light is cognized. Steady reminding of one's self of the true nature, behind body and personality, results in Self-remembering. Hence the advice: "Remember how it was with you before you forgot." And the Zen master's request of the student: "Show me your original face." Our real nature, before forgetting, was Pure Consciousness with no delusion. Our *original face* is Pure Consciousness.

46. **The knowledge produced by the realization of the true nature of Reality destroys immediately the ignorance characterized by the notions of "I" and "mine," as the**

light of the sun solves problems regarding directions mistakenly taken in the dark.

The notions of the ego-sense are caused, so sages declare, by the accumulated store of subconscious impressions carried over from the past. Until these are worked out, or neutralized, as long as one is in the body one will notice some obstruction to the flow of Divine Power. Therefore, either at physical death, when the karmic patterns are exhausted (and we are absorbed in the contemplation of the Absolute) or before physical death if karma is neutralized, we will be stable in the highest realization. Some teach that final liberation is possible only after the body and the subtle sheaths are discarded. Yet, if Supreme Consciousness is obviously free of entanglements, even though projecting the worlds, why can we not rest in the realization of the truth about life and still function through a body in this world?

47. The liberated soul endowed with complete enlightenment sees, through the eye of pure knowledge, the entire universe in his own Self and regards everything as the Supreme Consciousness (in manifestation) and nothing else.

A truly liberated person has no entanglements with any aspect of nature, even though he works within the framework of natural happenings. To be endowed means, in this instance, to be in firm possession of Knowledge, without any conflicting concept or opinion. Knowing the Self, which is the only Reality, a liberated person sees Consciousness as everything and everyone. The whole of manifest creation is then cognized as the body of Consciousness.

48. The tangible universe is verily Supreme Consciousness in manifestation; nothing whatsoever exists that is other

than Supreme Consciousness. As clay pots and jars cannot be anything but clay, so, to the enlightened person, all that is perceived is Pure Consciousness (in outward manifestation).

Supreme Consciousness is cause, and the universe is effect; the universe floats on a screen of consciousness and is said to be due to the imaginative intention of the Supreme. Just as cause and effect are one, so Supreme Consciousness and Its effect, are one. Only the appearances differ and the names differ.

49. The liberated soul, endowed with knowledge of the Supreme Consciousness, gives up the traits of his previous restricting characteristics. Because of his realization that he is of the nature of Existence-Knowledge-Bliss Absolute, he knows himself as Supreme Consciousness.

A person who is spiritually free while embodied, in possession of true Knowledge, ceases to identify with the traits characteristic of his prior limited lifestyle. He is no longer restrained by *maya* and lives under grace, always. When we are open to the flow of energy, and direction, which originates in the Transcendental Field, our life is lived not from an ego-sense but from the highest level. Here one can affirm, "I and Supreme Consciousness are one and the same." This does not mean that the embodied liberated person has control of the universal processes, but he knows he is a wave on the ocean; and the wave is the ocean *appearing as*.

50. A liberated soul, after crossing the ocean of delusion and rising above passion (and other feelings and urges which restrict), becomes one with peace and dwells in

the bliss derived from the realization of Supreme Consciousness alone.

Since peace and bliss are innate with Supreme Consciousness, one who is settled in the highest realization quite naturally is the embodiment of peace and bliss. This peace is not the kind of temporary stillness resulting from holding tendencies and urges at bay; it is the peace that surpasses human understanding. We are to rise above passion and move in a new and transcendent state of consciousness. To suppress powerful urges can be psychologically destructive. To channel energies properly and to refine the sensibilities is the far more creative approach. Also, to the degree that the transcendental experience is had, the passions and urges are transmuted.

51. Relinquishing attachment to illusory external happiness the Self-realized perfected being, satisfied with the bliss experienced in Supreme Consciousness, shines inwardly and thus illumines the world.

The average person is identified with sense-perceived things only, and his inner light flows out to cognize the world. A liberated person flows the searchlight of attention within and abides in the realization of the true nature. The worldly person's mind is darkened with sense impressions; the enlightened person's mind is illumined with the radiance of Consciousness. When, in the *New Testament,* we are admonished to, "Let that mind be in you which was in Christ Jesus," we are being invited to accept the power and the glory of Supreme Consciousness into our mental field, and very existence on earth. We can then know, "I am the light of the world." We do not speak of the personality, but of the manifesting Supreme Consciousness which is shining through the pure mental field of the master.

Self-Knowledge

52. Though associated with the restricting senses (and other aspects and attributes of nature). he, the contemplative one, is undefiled by their traits, clear like the sky, and he remains unmoved and unchanged under all conditions. He moves through life unattached.

Even though associated with body, mind and senses, the liberated person views these from the vantage point of the witness. He is, therefore, not restricted or deceived. Even when the body undergoes changes common to nature, such as aging and adjustments in body chemistry, a liberated person's consciousness is untouched. Nothing stays him from his appointed course of responsible action. He works always in harmony with natural laws and for the good of mankind and the world. Supreme Consciousness through him is able to carry out Its preordained plan of world enlightenment and planetary transformation. He dwells in the body for as long as the urgings of unspent karma demand; occasionally he will even remain longer, if work yet remains, by an act of Divinely personalized will.

53. Upon the dissolution of the restricting characteristics of the various bodies (sheaths) he, the contemplative one, is totally absorbed in Supreme Consciousness, which is all-pervading; like water in water, space is space and light in light.

Without the suggestion of individuality, after the momentum of subconscious impressions have been exhausted, the liberated person drops the body and all subtle sheaths and is again Supreme Consciousness without restriction; as before self-forgetting. If water is sealed in a container and submerged in water, when the container is opened, or broken, there will no longer be any separation of the water. Leaving the physical body does not alone insure liberation;

for the subtle sheaths and the mind can yet retain the soul's identification. But, when all "containers" are discarded, Supreme Consciousness is the Reality.

For a person to fear total awakening in Supreme Consciousness is as groundless as it is for a person who is dreaming, while asleep, to fear consciousness. It is not selfish of one to become Self-realized; it is the natural evolutionary trend. Some become Self-realized, and others do not. Some awaken partially and serve those who have yet to awaken, as guides and teachers of humanity. A few who are fully liberated remain in the body, not because of karma, but to do the will of God. That is, God works through available instruments and does as He wills to insure the orderly transformation of the world. A fully liberated soul, working on a God-sent mission, is referred to as an *avatara*, which means "the descent of divinity into flesh."

54. Realize that to be Supreme Consciousness, the attainment which leaves nothing more to be attained, the blessedness of which leaves no other bliss to be desired, and the knowledge of which, leaves nothing more to be known.

55. Realize that to be Supreme Consciousness which, when seen leaves nothing more to be seen, having become which one is not born again into the world of becoming, and which, when known, leaves nothing else to be known.

56. Realize that to be Supreme Consciousness which is Existence-Knowledge-Bliss Absolute, which is nondual and infinite, eternal and One, and which fills all the quarters—all that is above and below and all that exists in between.

57. Realize that to be Supreme Consciousness which is non-dual, indivisible, One, and blissful and which is indicated by the teachings of the seers as the irreducible substratum after the negation of all tangible objects.

In these verses the author affirms the highest truth in a manner which inspires and motivates. One feels an inner response to these affirmations because one *knows,* at the deepest level of being, that all that is affirmed is a certainty. Functioning at a level of even partial unknowing, there is yet more to be seen; having realized the Supreme Reality, however, one has seen all there is to see. The quest is at an end and one resides in Knowledge Itself. Having experienced the Reality, in contrast to the *reflection,* one is no longer born into the relative worlds; the worlds characterized by the trends of time, or becoming. Some sages teach students on the path: "God is ever-new, the realizations are never-ending." Yet, upon experiencing Pure Consciousness, there is nothing more to realize. Inherent in Pure Consciousness are bliss, timelessness and being. Awakening to the awareness of our real nature we know these to be our own essence. They are not modifications or characteristics, for Supreme Consciousness is without dualistic characteristics. This is incomprehensible to man, one who works through mind, but is the nature of Pure Consciousness.

58. Even the gods and goddesses taste only a particle of the unlimited bliss of Supreme Consciousness and enjoy, in proportion to their purity, their shares of that segment of bliss.

The "gods" and "goddesses" are said to be highly realized persons who have access to the *sphere of God.* This is the sphere of Supreme Consciousness with attributes, therefore, the totality of bliss is not "tasted" or enjoyed. We cannot divide Supreme Consciousness into segments, for it is indivisible, but to attempt an explanation we say that a portion of Supreme Consciousness manifests as the known universe; which is trillions of light years across. By our measurements the universe is not endless, it is bounded and space curves back upon itself. Yet, "outside" of space Pure Consciousness remains, as it remains "inside" of space. It is the basis, the substratum, the foundation of appearances; that is, of subtle and gross modifications of nature, the causes and the outer expression of forms.

The shining beings, even if without karma, are somewhat restricted by the modifications of their subtle vehicles; the causal organs of perception and action. Therefore, they cannot know the full Reality of Pure Consciousness. They are sometimes born into lower realms such as causal, astral and (sometimes) physical—in order to continue their works and participate in the stream of life.

59. All manifest objects are pervaded by Supreme Consciousness, all actions are possible because of It; therefore, Supreme Consciousness permeates everything but is not limited to the relationship.

The initial three aspects of Supreme Consciousness in manifestation are the triune characteristics of the Godhead: Existence; Consciousness-Intelligence; Energy flowing and cognized as Aum (Om, Amen), the Word, or Sound Current. At the positive pole of this initial magnetic field is the Existence aspect; God the Father, Brahma, or *Sat*. This aspect is stable and perfectly reflects Pure Consciousness, and is known as the highest, or most pure, Truth. At the negative pole of this initial magnetic field is the Creative Energy: The Holy Spirit, *Shiva*, whose nature is bliss *(ananda)* and is discerned as the Sound Current. Between the poles is "the first begotten of the Father," or Consciousness-Intelligence, the Christ Consciousness, *Vishnu*. The Holy Spirit *(Shiva)* aspect makes possible the production of the worlds by flowing outward as almost-pure energy, then becoming modified as various planes and dimensions. This process is under the intelligent direction of Consciousness, the Christ aspect or essence. The Existence aspect is stable and maintains everything else, as well as eventually draws the universes back into the Godhead. There is creation, or manifestation, preservation and dissolution of the worlds. This takes place time and time again as part of the cosmic process. We are told that this is taking place in "other times and other spaces" also. All persons of realization have known of this process as a result of direct inner perception, and have recorded their realizations which have become the great scriptures of the world. Seers and true prophets do not write to satisfy their own immature needs, for they have none; they write from inner realization, therefore, such scriptures are said to be "revealed truth" and is not the product of anyone's imaginings.

60. Realize that to be Supreme Consciousness which is neither subtle nor gross; neither short nor long; without birth and change; without form, qualities, or attributes.

61. Realize that to be Supreme Consciousness by the light of which luminous orbs like the suns and moons are illumined, but which cannot be illumined by *their* light, but, instead, is that by which everything is illumined.

Since Pure Consciousness is without attributes It is impossible to fully describe. Therefore, one approach is to state what It is *not*. After negating, or setting aside, all that It cannot be, It remains. Here, "qualities" refer to the three electric attributes, or *gunas* which pervade nature. Even though the moon, in this world, is illumined by the sun and the sun, by relative standards, has its own light, the sun could not exist if it were not for Supreme Consciousness. Therefore, the *Light* which makes possible all mundane lights is that of Pure Consciousness. No person has power of his own; his power has its origins in Pure Consciousness, flowing from the Godhead. This is why we say that there is One Power, One Presence, and One Being in the universe: God.

62. The Supreme Consciousness pervades the entire universe without and within and shines of Itself.

63. Supreme Consciousness is other than the manifest universe. There truly exists nothing that is not Supreme Consciousness. If any object appears to have independent reality it is an illusion, like a mirage reflected in heat waves.

This is the core of non-dualistic teaching. If this is understood, all else will be understood. One Thing exists: Supreme Consciousness. It is pure and it is impure; purity and impurity here does not relate to desirable or undesirable, good or bad, high or low, but to It being *without* attributes and *with* attributes. Without attributes It is Pure Supreme Consciouness; with attributes It is manifest as all that is. If we apply a name or label to an object and declare that it has independent existence, we are in error. The universe is not in error, it is not an illusion; *our faulty opinion of the universe is the basis for our own sense of illusion*. Therefore, like a mirage on a desert which is a reflection of something else, made possible by heat waves, what we see and touch is a reflection of something else, made possible by *maya* and our own faulty judgment. If we are not enlightened we tend to project, to assume, and draw conclusions based on faulty judgment and conditioned thought processes. The world we perceive is real in that it is Consciousness *appearing-as* we perceive it, but it is not what it seems to be to the ordinary sense perception.

64. **All that is perceived, all that is heard, is Supreme Consciousness (in manifestation) and nothing else. Attaining the knowledge of Reality, one sees the universe as the non-dual Supreme Consciousness.**

65. **Though Supreme Consciousness is Reality and is ever present everywhere, It is perceived by the eye of wisdom alone. But one whose vision is obscured by ignorance (and false perception) does not see the radiant Reality, as the blind do not see the resplendent sun.**

The truth about the Life Process cannot be totally known through the senses alone. One must use the "eye of wisdom," the faculty of discernment, if one is to know the truth. We might analyze the nature of the organic world and come to some understanding about the nature of the Life Process. We might turn within and perceive the subtle realms and, thereby, understand even more of the glory of creation. But this will still be the perception and apprehension of dualistic phenomena. Only when we see *through* the appearances to the Cause and Sustainer of it all, will we really be possessed of perfect knowledge. It is commonly believed that one can start where he is and gradually learn "more and more truth" until he works his way to final realization. Seers declare that it is possible for one to meditate correctly and discern the highest, or clearest, aspect of Life and, thereby, understand the entire cosmic process from the point of origin to the fullest outer expression. The *way of knowledge and wisdom* is not for the faint in heart, nor for the one lacking in courage. A seeker whose attitude is one of, "I will get there sometime," is not the ideal student to tread this path. There are other disciplines for those who are content to work in the realms of qualities and attritubes, and they are useful as preparation; to attune the mind and clear the accumulation of obstructing impressions.

66. The Self-realized soul, being purified in the fires of knowledge (arrived at by discipline, study and meditation) shines like gold.

The basic disciplines are for the purpose of clearing away obstructions of body and mind, transmuting energies into a more subtle essence, and directing attention to useful goals. Ideal study is that of contemplating the meaning behind the scriptures. One can use reason, if all data is known and the mind is well ordered, or one can use the contemplative process to discern truth. When unwanted matters are removed from gold, gold is then pure. When, through the fires of discipline, the undesirable qualities are removed from the consciousness of the seeker, he shines and is the visible organ of the resplendent Light.

67. Supreme Consciousness, which is the sun of knowledge, arises in the firmament of the heart and dissolves the darkness. The Pervader of all and the Sustainer of all, It illumines all as well as Itself.

The true source of light is Supreme Consciousness and is referred to as "the sun of knowledge." It reflects (arises) in the intellectual organ of the mind (the firmament of the heart) and darkness is immediately eradicated.

Self-Knowledge

68. He who, renouncing all (selfish) activities, worships in the sacred and stainless shrine of Supreme Consciousness, which is independent of time, place and distance; which is present everywhere; which is the destroyer of heat and cold and the other opposites; and which is the giver of eternal happiness, becomes all-knowing and all-pervading and attains immortality.

The shrine of Supreme Consciousness is the organ of discernment; without using discernment one will not be able to tell the difference between what is Real, versus what is the appearance. It is possible that one might also "worship" in the *crown chakra* and, thus, be swept into clear realization by the ascending energy flows. Liberation is natural to one who worships Supreme Consciousness with surrendered yearning, clear mental powers and total soul absorption.

SUMMATION

THE PATH OF SOUL LIBERATION

Teachers of the *way* have long spoken of the path which culminates in final realization. A path is commonly believed to lead to a destination; it also refers to a course of action, conduct, or procedure designed to assure the completion of a desired program. That desire plays a role in soul awakening is certain; yearning for Self-realization is characterized as one of the most important essentials if one is to know the Truth in this incarnation.

Another essential is Self-confidence; the confidence which springs from the inmost center of our being and which urges us to expend ourselves fully in order to move from mortal consciousness to the awareness of immortality. Without such confidence we are almost certain to wander through life in a confused manner, not sure of who we are, what to believe, or what to do with our alloted time on earth. We come to earth with unfinished business, with needs to satisfy and goals to reach. Seers advise us that our major reason for being here is to "work out our salvation" and become knowers of Truth. This *truth* of which they speak is "accurate comprehension of the nature of life." Centuries ago a nameless sage wrote: "Knowledge of evolution, life, and dissolution thus leads to complete emancipation from the bonds of *maya,* delusion. Beholding the self in the Supreme Self, man gains eternal freedom."

The paths are many, the realization is One. The names for Reality are many, the Reality Itself is One. We are not here concerned with any sectarian doctrine, for the essential message is the vital thread which runs through all living religious teachings. What we are concerned with is a clear and applicable system which will insure best results in the shortest possible time. We have all the time we need, to be sure, but persons intent upon Knowledge yearn for It and desire to experience It most quickly. This desire is not selfish and is the only one allowed a sincere seeker; all other desires lead to further entanglement in an ever-evolving world process. It must be said, however, that a willingness to serve this world process can, itself, be a way to soul liberation; if the surrender is complete and one is open to the flow of grace. We see grace in our lives when we are open to the unobstructed circulation of Divine Intent. Just as we have our duties, it is said that God has His; it is the regeneration of the material universe. Long ago the worlds were formed, as the creative energies were sent streaming from the Godhead into manifestation. In time, for *time* is a component of the basic material of which the worlds are formed, dormant energies stirred and "creation" became enlivened. Ever since, the manifest realms have been moving in the direction of "balance in God." Let no one be deceived on this point; there is a plan and a purpose behind what we sense and perceive.

We are participants in a cosmic drama. To refer to it as a game is to seem to make light of it; but, in a way, it is a game because there is a "script" and there are players on the stage. We are the players, the manifest realms are

Summation

the stage and the script has already been written. The universal happenings are not the result of a cosmic accident, but of cosmic design. We can, if we are willing, learn all about it and function creatively with the process. The decision is ours.

I have, for some time, wanted to write a commentary on "The way to Self-realization through Knowledge." Now I have done it, and this text can be used along with my earlier one dealing with the process of meditation, *This Is Reality*, based on the authoritative *Yoga-sutras*. Since my readers are English speaking, I have purposely done these works in English in order that the message might be communicated most effectively. Sanskrit is known as *Devangari*, "the language of the gods" and contains a potent *mantric* influence. Readers would do well to become acquainted with Sanskrit, but it is not essential to one if the inclination is not present. The science of *mantra* is based on sound and the influence of sound on surrounding spaces. Therefore, words which are correctly chosen mean what they imply and are not merely a matter of convenience. We shall touch on this a bit later in the text. Sanskrit was originally used in sacred temples as the teaching-language because it had a specific usage.

Shankaracharya and Self-Knowledge

Shankara was born, so legend has it, in A.D.788. He "withdrew" from this realm in the year A.D. 820; just thirty-two years old when he became invisible to mortal sight. He was a child prodigy and devoted himself to the practice of yoga and spiritual austerities at an early age. It was not long before his intellectual acumen was acknowledged by the leading philosophers of India. His mission was to reform the *Sanatana Dharma*, The Eternal Religion, and with that end in view he wrote commentaries on the principle scriptures of the time: the *Bhagavad Gita,* the *Brahma-sutras,* and the *Upanishads.* They are translated in many languages to this day and are considered to be the most accurate of all available renderings. *Acharya* means "the teacher who draws the student to the truth of the teaching" and *acharya* became affixed to Shankara's name. He was the "teacher of teachers." Of this, there can be no doubt. Traveling the length and breadth of India he bested all scholars and philosophers in the debates which were then popular. Before his final departure (it is not clear whether he retired into the Himalayan solitude, or actually left his body) he established major Centers of learning in the major quarters of India. Even today these Centers are headed by highly intelligent and realized men who trace their spiritual lineage back to Shankara; these four are the spiritual leaders of millions of devout Hindus.

Shankara also established the monastic order of swamis and assigned to it the leadership of society. It was felt that daily living should not be separated from philosophical study and application, that the vitality of spiritual insight should run through the entire social organism. Shankara lived at a time when Buddhism was beginning to lose influence and the teachers extant were themselves not capable of knowing or teaching, clear doctrine. Hinduism was beginning to reassert itself. Leadership was lacking and Shankara was a man for the times. Though he is often best known for such works as *Self-Knowledge,* he also wrote poems and hymns in praise of God so that people's faith could be stirred and their aspirations raised to new heights. One biographer describes him as the "unusual combination of philosopher and poet, savant and saint, mystic and religious reformer, debater of rare forensic power and passionate love of God."

Summation

It seems to me that Shankara must be considered as one of those rare beings who are sent to earth on a special mission. Perhaps he is an *immortal-mortal*, a forever-free soul whose destined path is that of remaining in proximity to the mundane realms in order to radiate beneficial influences. The great siddha, Babaji, first in my line of gurus, has stated that he gave *Kriya Yoga* initiation to Shankara many centuries ago. In recent times Babaji's most publicly known disciple was the Bengali master, Lahiri Mahasaya, who revived *Kriya Yoga* after centuries of neglect on the part of the average man. Through Lahiri's disciple, Swami Sri Yukteswar, Paramahansa Yogananda was trained to bring yoga teachings to the West.

It is taught, in the great religious books of the world, that whenever mankind needs a spiritual infusion then the Divine Power moves through a qualified and prepared person to restore the way of right living to the planet. Such persons are aware of their duty and desire nothing but to clear away the confusions which sometimes tend to settle in mass mind.

It is said that when Shankara was thirty-two years of age, and his work was completed, he retired into the Himalayas and there meditated; "absorbing his gross vehicles into the Self" he passed from this world. This does not mean that he dematerialized the various sheaths of the soul, but that he withdrew identification from them in true yogic fashion and became firmly established in the realization of Supreme Consciousness.

The Eternal Religion

No one can convert to *The Eternal Religion* because no one who lives up to the principles, regardless of present sectarian affiliation, is outside of the fold. *Sanatana Dharma* is the name given to this philosophilcal system by seers of the Vedas, thousands of years ago. Dharma is sometimes translated as "duty" or "prescribed conduct." It is also translated as "the natural order of things," or "the way of righteousness." Adherents of The Eternal Religion may practice any useful discipline and may hold to any useful belief about the relationship between God and the world; but always the understanding that One Thing supports the world is present.

This *way* is commonly, and mistakenly, referred to as Hinduism, sometimes Brahmanism. Both these words have been given by foreigners. The Sindhu river, flowing into the Arabian Sea and forming a part of the western boundary of India, was called the "Hindu" river by ancient Persians. The Greeks borrowed this name and changed it to "Indos," and later it was converted into the English "Indus." The inhabitants of that part of India then became known as Hindus, their religion as Hinduism. The people themselves prefer to call their religion The Eternal Religion, because it is based on the teachings of the Vedas and rests upon eternal, and realizable, principles. Therefore, the false impressions of this vital philosophical teaching are superimpostions attributed to outsiders who know little, or nothing, about the real message.

An understanding of the principles underlying the universal structure is essential to one who would be possessed of true Knowledge. One can remain a Christian, or a Buddhist, even an agnostic, and still study the principles of The Eternal Religion. Nothing could be more impractical than for one to hold to the beliefs of others who represent this philosophical system, without seeking out the basis for it all. Spiritual life cannot be a matter of pretense, or even sincere adaptation; the quest must be sincerely motivated and rightly pursued. There are thousands of Westerners

Summation

today who have identified outwardly with the cultural religious climate of India, who know next to nothing about either the roots or the Motive Power behind it.

The *Vedas* (from verb-root *vis*—to know) comprise a collection of hymns and teachings covering every area of philosophical speculation. They are considered to be "revealed truth" and no origin is known. The Vedas predate historical records. According to one scholar, an examination of certain Vedic texts reveals mention of an astronomical reference which would place that text at a point in time reckoned at 25,000 years B.C. Of course, from our modern point of view, antiquity does not necessarily mean a thing is valid; only if we *prove* the scriptures can we ever know for ourselves.

To analyze and search out the true meaning of the teaching has always been encouraged by Vedic seers. Blind faith is incompatible with Knowledge. Therefore, we are to study and probe, investigate and reason, meditate and strive for our own realization.

The Teaching

We view the world-process as a play of consciousness. Everything is taking place in time and space due to tension between the polarities of a huge magnetic field; the bounded universe. Supreme Consciousness shines upon the basic fabric of nature, *maya,* and the worlds are manifested. Shining upon the cosmic mental field the Godhead is expressed; shining upon the individualized mental fields souls become identified with bodies. The teaching is that One Thing appears as everything. Supreme Consciousness, the Reality, plays all the roles. It produces forms and ensouls forms. Our body, then, is Consciousness formed and we are reflections of Supreme Consciousness.

Since many do not consciously know their Real Nature they are in a temporary condition of unknowingness; they are ignorant of the Truth. But the Truth can be known, and this is the purpose of spiritual disciplines. Seers are consistent in their teaching relative to enlightenment; so long as we are content to identify merely with the outer realms we cannot hope to know the truth about the Universal, and That which supports outer manifestation. There is *one way;* we must "be born again." This second birth is the quickening of soul awareness which is the beginning of the spiritual quest, the urge for Knowledge of the highest order. We are born into this world so that we might learn how not to be compulsively born again; we "die" to the world so that we might never have to die again.

After energy flows out from the Godhead to produce the gross realms, a portion of this energy remains dormant and acts as an anchor to keep matter settled. This secret, hidden, subtle, or *potential* force is *kundalini*. It is what ties us to the body. Being identified with the body we assume that we are a body. This assumption is false. There are at least two ways for us to experience freedom, or perfect Knowledge: we can use our faculty of discernment to determine which is our Real Nature versus the conditioned one; and we can experience the awakening of *kundalini* and flow with it as it ascends back to the *crown chakra*. Some teachers stress one way over the other, but there is no reason why both cannot coincide. In fact, they usually do.

Some work with the energies and use little, or no, discernment. Theirs then tends to be an emphasis upon feeling and experience. Others emphasize discernment and they tend to remain stable on the path and are less likely to lose their way. In either discipline the presence of a qualified spiritual guide is almost always essential. To be *qual-*

Summation

ified the teacher must be an expert, one who has himself experienced fulfillment. He must be pure in motive and have as his only interest, where the student is concerned, the student's spiritual welfare. In these days of widespread interest in philosophical matters and easy access to superfical information, there are many teachers who are not, themselves, Self-realized and many students who are not yet fully committed to the path. In this matter of spiritual discipline "good intentions" are not sufficient; what is needed is accurate information and correct application of the principles.

Unless he is born with Knowledge a guru will be a disciple of a known guru, and the line can be traced back for centuries. There are rare instances where a seeker is instructed in a vision, or a dream, but the most obvious type of instruction is from a person who is present in the body. In this way communication between teacher and student is likely to be more accurate and meaningful. The guru is the guide, the teacher, and the one whose state of consciousness elevates those who come into his presence. A guru is aware that he is but a visible instrument of the Divine. He knows Supreme Consciousness to be the true guru; he is but an outer representative. Therefore, the seeker should pray and yearn for Knowledge and not look to any outside source. When the time is ripe, if it is destined in this incarnation, God in the form of the guru will come into the seeker's life. This is a never-failing process and is the usual way in which the doctrine is transmitted.

One is not required to forsake daily responsibilities and social duties in order to seek Knowledge; what is required is that one discriminate between what is important and what is not important, what is useful and what is not useful. Rather than escape the world before karmic ties are dissolved, one is advised to *perform one's duty* with the right attitude. When we are open to the flow of Spiritual Energy we are instruments through which grace can express in our lives. In this way the worlds are transformed and the Divine Intention is more adequately fulfilled.

Our universe is described by seers as a full manifestation of Consciousness, and seven specific spheres, or levels, are designated. They are: *the sphere of God*, the first self-modification of Supreme Consciousness, with attributes; *the sphere of the Holy Spirit*, the expressive aspect of the Godhead; *The sphere of Spiritual Reflection*, where the sense of separation begins; *the sphere of Maya*, the connecting point, or door between higher and lower realms; *the sphere of Magnetic Auras*, the realm of subtle organs and causes; *the sphere of Electric Attributes*, the astral realm; *the sphere of Material Substance*, the physical universe. The Sanskrit term for each sphere is *loka*, thus from subtle to gross we have: *Satyaloka, Tapoloka, Janaloka, Maharloka, Swarloka, Bhuvarloka, and Bhuloka.*

The way to Self-Knowledge is through these spheres which screen Truth from our perceptions. One who is firmly identified with the lower spheres usually does not even know of the existence of the higher ones, and even if he learns of them he does not truly know through experience. Knowing *about* the Life Process is not the same as *knowing* It.

Within the human body are seven major centers through which vital forces are distributed. They are known as *chakras*, and correspond to the levels of consciousness which make possible comprehension of, and access to, the above mentioned spheres. I have written at greater length concerning the *chakra* system in two of my other books, *The Way of the Initiate* and *Darshan: The Vision of Light*.

Since most persons have difficulty with uncontrolled thoughts in the early stages of meditation, and often cannot

Summation

move from one level of awareness to another for lack of a process, certain meditation techniques have been evolved which are useful. They do not rely upon one's belief in the efficacy of the method, but upon proper and regular practice. One of these techniques is *mantra,* which is basic to almost all mystical disciplines regardless of cultural origins. The highest *mantra* is Om, or Aum; other *mantras* derive from this Primal Sound. A *mantra* can serve many purposes depending upon the design and application. Mantras for specific purposes usually contain a *seed* concept, or the sound used is planned to produce a definite effect. Therefore, such *mantras* need to be learned from a qualified *mantra* teacher so that the correct intention and sound-quality is utilized. Otherwise they will not be effective. We can influence the subtle subtances in surrounding space by playing certain music or intoning certain sounds. The effect of sound on the nervous system is well known; also sound can activate the *chakras* and awaken their sleeping potency. When a teacher gives a *mantra* to a student it is given with the teacher's insight and infused with his intention, then the *mantra* is truly a sound with power to influence. The right use of *mantra* can also be used to awaken *kundalini*.

Songs, or chants in any language, can be used as *mantras* if correctly used with an understanding of intonation and repetition. They should not have a hypnotic effect, but should result in a clearing of mind and consciousness. A well-known *mantra* is the *maha* (great) *mantra:* "Hari Rama, Hari Rama, Rama, Rama, Hari, Hari—Hari Krishna, Hari Krishna, Krishna, Krishna, Hari, Hari." The chanting of this phrase, with the correct devotional emphasis, has a powerful cleansing effect on the subtle system. Others are *hong-sau* and *so-ham* mantra. There are many which are known and used with benefit. A *mantra* one can use, with the *intention* to know, is "I am Pure Consciousness." These are not affirmations used to condition the subconscious level of mind, they are statements used to enable us to awaken to the Truth. A Sanskrit *mantra* is often first intoned verbally, then inwardly, then mentally, then it continues by itself. This final and more subtle happening is the purest use of *mantra,* for it then begins to act upon deeper layers of our nature and leads awareness to the edge of Pure Consciousness. When the *mantra* ceases automatically and if we have practiced correctly, the transcendental experience is naturally ours.

In a Vedic text we read: "*Aum* is heard through the cultivation of the heart's natural love, moral courage, memory of one's divinity, and true concentration which leads to the transcendental experience." We can listen to the internal sound of *Aum* by directing attention to the *crown chakra* and listening within. In time we will hear sounds of a physical nature, then subtle sounds emanating from the *chakra system,* then the Word Itself. *Aum* flows from the *crown chakra* and changes in frequency as it moves downward through the other vital centers. Directing our attention to the *crown chakra* we finally become attuned to the pure sound of *Aum,* then flowing with It we are led back to the point of origin within us. The *crown chakra* corresponds to the Godhead, therefore, one who is established at this highest center can easily comprehend the nature of God. Self-realization automatically assures God-realization.

A student is taught by the teacher according to the capacity of the student; the methods advised will be useful to the individual only if correctly prescribed. There should be no hesitation on the part of a seeker to ask for guidance from a qualified teacher. But the teacher can only instruct, encourage and assist with his blessings; the student must do the work for himself. While a guru will encourage attunement, he will not encourage dependency, for this would weaken the student instead of calling forth his innate potential.

Teaching traditions vary but they have a common purpose. My line of gurus, for instance, teach a synthesis of yoga practice and offer a system useful to the individual. At initiation the student is instructed in the practice of *Kriya Yoga,* a combined series of meditation techniques designed to awaken *kundalini,* purify the nervous system and make meditation fruitful. This *Kriya Yoga* system includes instruction in matters of philosophy, techniques to regulate the circulation of vital force, *mantra* and the most effective meditation procedures. Before initiation the student is instructed in matters of attitude, behavior and work habits. Except in rare instances, most of us are to live in the world and make our contribution to the evolutionary process; at the same time we are advised to attend to our spiritual practices. It is not true that one who lives in seclusion has more time to give to self-discipline; regardless of our station in life we can face matters with the correct attitude and schedule our time in order to accomplish important tasks. Therefore, *the path of liberation* is for all persons, regardless of who they are, or what their role in life happens to be.

Balance is required of us if we would succeed on the spiritual path in this incarnation. We are to see to the health and proper function of our body, the maintenance of our environment, the welfare of those dependent upon us and to the nourishment of the world as nature. We are also to train ourselves emotionally and mentally, for without emotional health and a strong mind we cannot stand the rigors of intensive meditation and self-analysis. In time now gone by, one could not even hope for initiation into the finer points of meditation and Self-discovery until necessary preliminary training had been concluded to the satisfaction of the teacher. We are to root out negative tendencies and encourage the positive ones. We are to so discipline our lives that we expend our energies and utilize our time for specific and useful purposes. It may be that some health deficiencies may be compensated for by the possession of emotional balance and a well-ordered mind; but it is certain that without stability and without a clear, and well-ordered, mind one is not suited for advanced stages of meditation.

We need not involve ourselves in a frantic search for a Master to learn how to observe the virtues and how to properly use the mental faculties; we have only to turn to the nearest scripture, of any Faith, to be reminded of the guidelines. For encouragement we may need occasional contact with those stronger than ourselves, but this contact should be for encouragement and reinforcement so that we learn to stand firmly on our own. The same Power and Intelligence which brought the universe into expression and which has brought us to our present station in life, will see to it that we are led in the proper paths once our life has been surrendered completely. When we are ready, and if we require it, we will be led to a teacher, or a teaching-situation, which will provide us with the necessary impetus to reach the goal. This is the way the Principle works.

I know of no fast way to enlightenment; the disciplines required are of the most arduous nature, and become more subtle as we progress. No sooner have we conquered one habit than another, more subtle than the one before, looms before us. No sooner have we overcome one major temptation, than another more enticing than before, presents itself. As we go along we are often horrified to find that our understanding is not as pure as we thought it was, and there are decisions to be made which leave us in a quandary; here, only surrender and the activity of grace will enable us to continue. One teacher, in summing up this phase of the quest said: "The way is strewn with broken glass."

All true teachings have an outer, and an inner, message. The outer message is for the masses and for general encouragement and guidance for all persons. The inner, or esoteric, message is for those who are possessed of special qualities and who are fit for the challenge of probing the most secret recesses of consciousness. This exposition on Self-Knowledge is for the few who are possessed of those special qualities; but others will also derive benefit from careful and repeated study. In the *Bhagavad Gita* Krishna speaks: "Out of a thousand, one seeks Me; out of a thousand who thus seek, one knows Me as I truly am." This would seem to narrow the field to but a few, but it is also a prod to greater effort, for if even one person out of a million experiences Self-realization, then each has a chance. Out of all our associates who claim to be on the spiritual path, how many do we know who are truly disciplined and truly dedicated? We should not judge from outward appearances, of course, for the major point is are *we* truly disciplined and truly dedicated? Do we do the best we can regardless of what others think of us? If we are "hidden with Christ, in God" we have no reason to be concerned about the opinions of others.

It is possible to live in Eternity while yet functioning in a three-dimensional world. Those who are yet in worldly consciousness do not understand this, but it is a possibility. Age after age, cycle after cycle, the outer pattern of life rises and falls; behind the scenes, Pure Consciousness remains ever the same. Our ultimate destiny is to learn to live *consciously,* with *total understanding.* All it takes is a yearning for Knowledge, discipline of the highest order, and the correct use of the faculty of discernment. This is the message of the seers. This is the message of the supremely free beings who invite us into the realization of Supreme Consciousness.

GLOSSARY

Advaita—Non-duality; the teaching that God, soul, and the universe are One. Known as *Vedanta*; the final summing up of the Vedic philosophy.

ahamkara—One of the functions of the inner organ of perception; Ego, or "I" consciousness.

ajnana—Meaning either individual, or cosmic, ignorance. This alone is the cause of false perception and our sense of multiplicity.

akasa—Often spelled "akasha"; the first of five material elements making up nature; sometimes translated as "space" or "ether."

Ananda—Bliss; often used as part of the monastic name of those in the swami order. For instance, Yogananda; "Bliss through yoga, or divine union."

anandamayakosa—The initial sheath, or covering of the soul.

annamayakosa—The physical body.

antahkarana—The inner organ of the soul's perception when operating in time and space; comprising mind, intellect or faculty of discernment, ego, and the tendency towards pleasure.

Atmabodha—Self-Knowledge; and the title of this treatise by Shankara.

avatara—The "descent" of Divinity into flesh; an Incarnation of God in human form; a Savior, or World Redeemer.

avidya—Same as *ajnana* (see above).

Bhagavad Gita—A brief eighteen-chapter work; "The Song of God." One of the central scriptures of India, seting forth the dialogue which takes place betwen Krishna (an incarnation of the Divine) and Arjuna (the seeker on the path of yoga).

Brahma—The first person of the Trinity in Hindu thought; the same as "God the Father" of the Christians.

Brahmachari—A self-disciplined student who devotes himself to spiritual practices under a guru, or competent teacher.

Brahmaloka—The abode of God; corresponding to the highest heavenly plane of Christians and other dualistic religionists.

Brahman—The Supreme Reality, the Absolute without attributes or qualities.

Brahma-sutras—Also known as Vedanta-sutras; a treatise on high philosophical views and a central scrpiture for knowledge-oriented students.

Brahmavidya—The knowledge of Supreme Consciousness.

Buddha—The Enlightened One; the founder of Buddhism. The Buddha was Indian; later his teachings migrated to Tibet, China and all of Asia. Hinduism and Buddhism,

Glossary

of all of the world's religions, have the largest number of adherents.

buddhi—The faculty of discernment, or determination; sometimes translated as "intellect," that which makes decisions.

Chit—Consciousness.

devas—The gods, or "shining ones" who function at subtle levels and in more rarified planes.

Govinda—One of the names of Krishna

Govindapada—One of the great teachers and guru of Shankara.

guna—The *qualities*, or electric attributes in nature. *Tamas guna* stands for inertia or heaviness; *Rajas guna* is the neutralizing current and is sometimes referred to as the active quality; *Sattva guna* promotes righteousness and upliftment.

guru—A popular definition is "teacher." A precise definition is "that which dispells darkness." A true guru, being enlightened and knowing the way to Self-Knowledge is qualified to guide the sincere seeker on the path.

Isvara—Or, Iswara; the personal aspect of God which governs, or regulates, the universe. Supreme Consciousness in modified expression for the purpose of directing the cosmic activity.

japa—Reciting a mantra or divine name. *See* mantra.

jivanmukta—Liberation while embodied, a "free soul."

jnana—The knowledge of the Life Process. Jnana Yoga is the way of highest knowledge.

Kapila—The author of one of the great Indian systems of philosophy.

karma—Action; sometimes translated as "duty," for instance, "It is my karma to do this work." Also, used in the explanation of causes and effects.

kosa—Sometimes spelled "kosha," a sheath, or covering. The five coverings of the soul: the physical body; the astral, or vital body; the mental sheath; the covering of the organ of intelligence; and the sheath of bliss, or most subtle soul-envelope.

Krishna—Considered to be a Divine Incarnation; the central character in the *Bhagavad Gita* and other epic works. Considered to be a Vishnu Avatar; an Incarnation of the preservation-aspect of the Godhead who restores "the way of righteousness."

kundalini—Dormant, or static, vital force resting in nature; when it awakens in nature then life emerges on a planet; when it awakens in man then the soul begins the journey through inner space in the direction of Self-Knowledge.

Mahadeva—A name for Shiva (Siva); a literal translation is, "great (maha) god (deva)."

manomayakosa—The sheath of the mind.

mantra—Sound which has a specific influence on ether, used to focus attention and arouse dormant energies and qualities.

maya—A term used to denote delusion; specifically it is the "stuff" of which the worlds are framed. The components are: time, space, light particles, and energy. It has two characteristics: it is that which veils the truth from the soul by clouding the faculties of perception; it is form-building, and makes possible the production of forms in time and space.

Glossary

moksha — Freedom, or liberation.

Nirguna Brahman — Supreme Consciousness without attributes, the Absolute.

Nirvana — To "blow out"; the eradication of all that prevents Self-Knowledge, the result is liberation.

nirvakalpa samadhi — The clear realization of Supreme Consciousness with no sense of difference and no mental support.

Om — The Sound Current; *pranava, aum, or Amen*. The sound of the creative energies flowing from the Godhead. The primal sound from which all sound variations emerge, and into which they are return.

Patanjali — Considered to be the author of the *Yoga-sutras;* the authoritative work on Raja Yoga, the way of discipline, mind control, concentration and *samadhi*.

Prakriti — The material realms, consisting of the elements and electric attributes, or qualities.

prana — The primal energy; vital force.

pranamayakosa — The vital body, or astral sheath.

prarabdha karma — Subconscious impressions which are now beginning to be worked out in this incarnation.

Purusha — The Conscious Principle; this, in union with the subtle elements of the material realms results in the production of the universe.

rajas — The principle of activity, or neutralization. *Rajasic;* pertaining to this principle.

rishi — A seer of Reality; one who reveals the wisdom of the scriptures.

Saguna Brahman — Supreme Consciousness with attributes; The Godhead, with three aspects.

samadhi—When the waves of the mind cease, "oneness" is experienced. There can be "union" with an object contemplated, or there can be unrestricted Being.

samsara—The relative worlds, which are forever changing, evolving and moving in the direction of eventual dissolution. Since the *gunas* pervade matter, one who is identified with matter is caught up in the process of forever change.

Sanatana Dharma—*The Eternal Religion.* The true religion of the Hindus, and all who seek out the highest truth. It can be traced back to pre-Vedic times and is said to be without origin; having been always known to a few, and directly revealed to initiate seers.

Sankaracharya—*Shankaracharya,* or *Shankara;* India's great exponent of Non-dualistic philosophy.

sannyasa—The monastic life, dedicated to Self-realization and world service.

sannyasi—One who renounces worldly concerns in order to devote time and energy to Self-Realization.

sattva—The uplifting, or elevating principle in nature.

savikalpa samadhi—Union with God, or an attribute of God, in which the distinction between subject and object is present.

shakti—Creative energy which animates the worlds; creative energy circulating through the organism after kundalini has awakened.

siddha—A "perfect being"; one who has become established in Knowledge through yoga practice, or any discipline which results in Self-realization. A spiritual master; qualified to be a true guru and whose presence can awaken kundalini in the seeker who is attuned.

Siva—Shiva: The third person of the Hindu Trinity, or the Holy Spirit.

*Sushumna—*The passage in the spinal canal through which kundalini ascends. At seven places in the astral cerebrospinal system are the *chakras:* base chakra; sacral chakra; lumbar chakra; dorsal chakra; cervical chakra; third-eye chakra; and crown chakra. Vital force descends from the top and is distributed through the chakras, or *wheels:* viewed as circular masses of light they are varied as to color and sound-emanations.

*Turiya—*The "fourth" state of consciousness; transcending the three states of waking, dream, and deep sleep.

*Upanishads—*A section of the Vedas which are considered an important collection of scripture. There is said to be one hundred and eight Upanishads, and eleven are considered to be the most important.

*Vedanta—*The summing up of the essence of the Vedas.

*Vedas—*The scriptures setting forth The Eternal Religion. Occult historians claim that the "light of the Vedas" has filtered down through Esoteric Buddhism in Asia, and the Esoteric Traditions of the Middle East and Europe, thereby lending vitality to all major world religions.

*Vishnu—*A name for the preserver aspect of the Godhead; the Second Person of the Trinity, or the Christ. Jesus would be considered, as was Krishna, as an Incarnation of the aspect of the Godhead whose duty it was to restore order, inspire the masses, and establish virtue.

*viveka—*Discrimination. For instance, *Vivekananda* means "bliss through discrimination; between the Real and the transitory."

*Vyasa—*A sage who is believed to have arranged the Vedas

in their present form. Legend has it that the name refers to several sages, who appeared at successive times, to continue the work started by earlier philosophers.

yoga—To "yoke" or join together; union with God. *Savikalpa samadhi* is the goal of yoga practice; *nirvikalpa samadhi* is the *Transcendental Experience*.

Recommended Supplemental Study

The following books by Roy Eugene Davis will be useful in conjunction with the one you are now reading.

This Is Reality A commentary based on the *yoga-sutras*.
$3.95

The Way of the Initiate Man's true origin, nature and spiritual destiny. $3.00

Darshan The Vision of Light Instruction on yoga, and the author's training under Paramahansa Yogananda.
$3.95

The Bhagavad Gita The verses of this classic scripture have been paraphrased in English, with commentary.—$3.00

Obtain these titles from your bookseller,
or from the publisher:
CSA Press
Lakemont, Georgia
30552

Information on the Spiritual Awareness Home Study Course, recordings, and other books by the author will be sent free on request.